D0776871

The Wisdom of Children

A Book of Quotes from and about Kids

The Wisdom of Children

A Book of Quotes from and about Kids

Edited by Carol Kelly-Gangi

BARNES
& NOBLE
BOOKS
NEW YORK

ACKNOWLEDGMENTS

My heartfelt thanks to the many children who contributed to this book. I thank you for the honesty, wisdom, and humor of your answers. And special thanks to all of the parents who were gracious enough to compile their children's answers— your time and efforts are greatly appreciated.

The quotes in this book have been drawn from many sources, and are assumed to be accurate as quoted in their previously published forms. Although every effort has been made to verify the quotes and sources, the publisher cannot guarantee their perfect accuracy.

2004 Barnes & Noble Books

ISBN 0-7607-6210-4

Printed and bound in the United States of America

04 05 06 07 08 HC 9 8 7 6 5 4 3 2 1

For John Christopher
with love

Introduction

DIPLOMACY MAY NOT BE ONE OF A CHILD'S STRONG suits. Children tend to tell it like it is—spouting out the unvarnished truth as only they can express it. But what they say often cuts to the heart of a matter, and displays a wisdom, honesty, and wit that far surpasses the age of the speaker.

The Wisdom of Children is a book of more than 250 quotations from and about kids. In it, kids let loose on a variety of subjects such as parents, love and marriage, politicians, what grown-ups can learn from kids, what they wish for, and how they hope the world will change when they grow up. There are also some mixed-up facts on the subjects of religion, science, and history that could have only been conceived by the mind of a child.

You'll also find selections from some former kids as well. What parent hasn't experienced the barrage of questions that children ask? Or the occasional embarrassing moment at something one of their kids said in public? Contributors such as Bill Cosby, Vicki Iovine, Art Linkletter, Fred Rogers, and Philip Roth share lively anecdotes on these topics. While contributors as diverse as Deepak Chopra, Charles Dickens, Ralph Waldo Emerson, Mick Jagger, Anne Tyler, and George F. Will offer selections that speak to the simple joy and wonder of children and what they teach us.

So forget what your parents told you about kids being seen and not heard. The next time your child pipes up to tell you something, take a moment and listen—it may be a pearl of wisdom after all.

—Carol Kelly-Gangi
Rumson, NJ 2004

Kids Talk About Moms

What makes someone a good Mom?

A good mom is always there when you need a hug. She's just like a best friend.

—JESSICA, age 12

They take care of you when you have a boo-boo. They kiss it and clean up your toys and they give you lots of stuff for your birthday. They do a lot of hard work for you.

—DANIELLE, age 5

Moms are the spoonful of sugar that helps the medicine go down.

—DEBORAH, age 17

Sometimes they have to say yes and sometimes they have to say no.

—BAILEY, age 6

She cares about me, gets me everything, and gives me private time in the bathroom.

—JUSTIN, age 4

Someone who is sweet, kind, generous, forgiving and cares about their kids' health and safety.

—ELIZABETH, age 12

She helps me clean up and we do fun things together.

—JACK, age 4

Mothers are like water; they help you grow. Without them you would wither and die; but too much water will always kill a flower.

—CASSIE, age 16

Someone who feeds you good things, takes care of you, is thoughtful and kind, and is always there for you.

—MADISON, age 9

A good mommy spends a lot of time with her kids.

—AVERY, age 6

If they don't yell that much, then they are a good mom.... I personally think that what makes a good mom is they're nice, they give lots of hugs (my mom does that a lot). And if they make good food (my mom does that too).

—BEN, age 9

She's someone that helps you with your homework. Someone who can handle arguments.

—MICHAEL, age 8

They help their kids get healthy. If they throw up or something, they always take care of them.

—ROSIE, age 6

They take you to the mall.

—BRENNA, age 11

They give you hugs and kisses.

—EMILY, age 6

She loves me a lot.

—BENJAMIN, age 7

Kids Talk About Dads

What makes someone a good Dad?

If they always play with you, and always give you the right amount of attention.

—BENJAMIN, age 8

They do stuff for their children like help them put on their pjs.

—AMANDA, age 5

Someone who teaches you sports.

—PATRICK, age 11

A daddy who is really good at being the tickle monster.

—AVERY, age 6

He wrestles with me, loves me, and sends me letters and stuffed scorpions from Kuwait!

—JUSTIN, age 4

He helps me type stuff on the computer.

—BENJAMIN, age 7

Only a father would ride on the roller coaster with me, come off with a green face and say he had a good time.

—LONI, age 11

A dad is somebody who can get away with doing things he tells you not to do.

—PAUL, age 14

When dads say "yes" to everything.

—BRENNA, age 11

They wash you, they put your games on the computer, they go to work to make money for our house and to buy us food.

—DANIELLE, age 5

He gets good toys for me and brings me to the beach and arcade.

—JACK, age 4

I give hugs to my Daddy. He gives kisses to me.

—MARY, age 3

He buys us stuff.

—EMILY, age 6

A dad who has a good sense of humor and likes having fun with his children.

—ALENA, age 8

He's someone that can control his temper.

—MICHAEL, age 8

A good dad is someone who can balance work and taking care of his family.

—CAMERON, age 13

Kids on Love and Marriage

Years ago when I was first planning Disneyland, I asked one of my teenage daughters what I could add to the park to make it especially interesting to girls her age. "Boys," she replied without missing a beat.

—WALT DISNEY

Little boy to playmate as a pretty girl passes by: "Boy! If I ever stop hating girls, she's the one I'll stop hating first!"

—ANONYMOUS

If falling in love is anything like learning how to spell, I don't want to do it. It takes too long.

—GLENN, age 7

I'm not rushing into being in love. I'm finding fourth grade hard enough.

—REGINA, age 10

If you want to be loved by somebody who isn't already in your family, it doesn't hurt to be beautiful.

—ANITA, age 8

Be a good kisser. It might make your wife forget that you never take out the trash.

—DAVE, age 8

It's better for girls to be single but not for boys. Boys need somebody to clean up after them!

—ANITA, age 9

Dates are for having fun, and people should use them to get to know each other. Even boys have something to say if you listen long enough.

—LYNNETTE, age 8

Christians have only one spouse. This is called monotony.

—ANONYMOUS CHILD

When is it okay to kiss someone?

The rule goes like this: If you kiss someone, then you should marry them and have kids with them. It's the right thing to do.

—HOWARD, age 8

If it's your mother, you can kiss her anytime. But if it's a new person, you have to ask permission.

—ROGER, age 6

When they're rich.

—PAM, age 7

When someone is feeling sad and when you see a relative. By kissing them you show them that you really love them.

—DANIELLE, age 5

You should never kiss a girl unless you have enough bucks to buy her a big ring and her own VCR, 'cause she'll want to have videos of the wedding.

—Jim, age 10

The law says you have to be eighteen, so I wouldn't want to mess with that.

—Curt, age 7

It's never okay to kiss a boy. They always slobber all over you...that's why I stopped doing it.

—Tammy, age 7

How does someone decide who to marry?

No person really decides before they grow up who they're going to marry. God decides it all way before, and you got to find out later who you're stuck with.

—KIRSTEN, age 10

Not by how they look, but by how kind they are.

—BENJAMIN, age 8

They meet each other and he asks you if you want to go out and you say yes. After you've been out on a few dates, he asks you to marry him and you say yes.

—ROSIE, age 6

You look for all the qualities you want in a partner. You make sure that you both want children or not.

—MACKENZIE, age 10

It isn't always just how you look. Look at me. I'm handsome like anything and I haven't got anybody to marry me yet.

—BRIAN, age 7

If they really, truly love each other.

—ALEXANDER, age 12

Because they think they are a good person and they love them.

—CAROLINE, age 6

They date 'em for a long time. You decide if you really want to get married, then the boy proposes and she says yes. Then they get married.

—LILY, age 9

If you know somebody who has lots of stuff in common with you.

—AVERY, age 6

Someone decides who they should marry when they're in love. They have a feeling they can't describe. They see themselves together in 50 years.

—CAMERON, age 15

The boy and girl are in love. When they get married they have a little boy and girl and they are so happy to have them.

—DANIELLE, age 5

First they have to go on a lot of dates together, talk and solve problems.

—MADISON, age 9

You have to talk to them first and then bring them over to your house.

—CRISTIAN, age 6

If they look good.

—BENJAMIN, age 7

Hmm. OK. That's a bit tougher. I'm only 8, so I shouldn't know yet.

—MICHAEL, age 8

What do you think your Mom and Dad have in common?

They take care of the little ones. They both clean up. They both love us the same. When they fight, they always make up.

—DANIELLE, age 5

They like to talk together, walk together, and bike ride.

—BAILEY, age 6

They laugh together.

—MICHAEL, age 15

They both like ice cream.

—EMILY, age 7

They are both lawyers.

—MICHAEL, age 8

They are both funny.

—PATRICK, age 11

They both have cars.

—EMILY, age 6

They yell a lot.

—BRENNA, age 11

They both like chocolate and they like to go out together.

—AVERY, age 6

They agree with each other.

—CAROLINE, age 6

They are both nice and they like to dance. They love being in the outdoors and kissing together.

—MADISON, age 9

My mom and dad are both responsible parents, who take care of us and don't lay around the house.

—ALENA, age 8

My parents have nothing in common. They're divorced.

—JESSICA, age 12

They're both really good parents. They love each other and their children. They both look good.

—LILY, age 9

They both love me.

—BENJAMIN, age 7

Questions, Questions, and more Questions

"Mister Rogers! How did you get out of the box?" That's what a young boy asked when he met me. I told him that I'm a real person and that I live in a real home with my family, not in the television. He nodded all through my explanation, and then asked, "But how are you going to get back into the box?"

—FRED ROGERS, TV personality and educator

Dialogue between mother and five-year-old who's in the next room:

"Mommy, can I eat this candy I found on the floor?"

"No, there are germs on it."

Slight pause.

"Mommy, can I eat it now? I licked all the germs off."

—ART LINKLETTER, entertainer and writer

During this past Christmas while I was on a shopping spree in a department store I heard a little five-year-old talking to his mother on the down escalator. He said, "Mommy, what do they do when the basement gets full of steps?"

—HAL LINDEN, actor

Little boy crying to a sales clerk in a large department store: "Have you seen a lady without a kid that looks just like me?"

—EVA SHAW, writer and educator

28

During a walk, my four-year-old son saw someone with a dog and asked me if he could pet it. I said he could, as long as he asked first. So he walked up to the dog and said, "Is it okay if I pet you?"

—GISELLE LEBLANC, quoted in *Parents* magazine

After she stepped in dog dirt and proceeded to track it all through the car, my young daughter turned to my husband and me and said, "But how did the dog get into our car?"

—GWEN KELLY, mother of five

I was expecting my second child, and my five-year-old son, Marcus, was full of questions, "What does the baby do in your belly?" he asked, "Well," I explained, "The baby eats, sleeps and waits to be born." He looked at me, then hurried off. Returning, he handed me one of his little toys and said, "Here, Mom, swallow this so the baby won't be bored."

—ANONYMOUS MOM

I used to get frantic when my first two kids got to be about age three and asked the inevitable question, "Where do babies come from, Mommy?" Immediately the room would spin and in the maelstrom I would try to carefully put together an explanation that was both age appropriate and factual. It was only by my third and fourth kids that I learned the answer that was most satisfying to a three-year-old and a three-year-old's mom: "From the hospital, honey."

—VICKI IOVINE from
The Girlfriends' Guide to Toddlers

We were so excited to tell our three-year-old about the new baby who was to be born into the family. She caught us completely off guard when she asked, "Who will be that baby's mommy?"

—FRED ROGERS, TV personality and educator

It's a family joke that when I was a tiny child I turned from the window out of which I was watching a snowstorm, and hopefully asked, "Momma, do we believe in winter?"

—PHILIP ROTH, novelist

One night while we were watching election news, my 5-year-old daughter, Katherine, asked what all the signs were for. I explained that a man was running for president and the signs said to vote for him. She asked, "So the person who runs the fastest wins?"

—THERESA PETUSKY, quoted in *Parents* magazine

What Kids Have Learned

You should never laugh at your dad if he's mad or screaming at you.

—JOHN, age 12

When your dad is mad and asks you, "Do I look stupid?" don't answer him.

—HEATHER, age 16

If your sister hits you, don't hit her back. Parents always catch the second person.

—MICHAEL, age 10

Never trust a dog to watch your food.

—PATRICK, age 10

Don't think life is easy, because when you get older it is hard work. I used to think life was easy, now I have to do the dishes every other day.

—NICK, age 9

Don't bite the hand that has your allowance in it.

—ANONYMOUS CHILD

Never tell your mom her diet's not working.

—MICHAEL, age 14

If you put your brother's hand in warm water, he *will* wet the bed.

—ELIZABETH, age 12

Sleep in your clothes so you'll be dressed in the morning.

—STEPHANIE, age 8

Stay away from prunes.

—RANDY, age 9

It is better to read the book than the Cliffs Notes.

—LAURA, age 16

You should never mess with a kid that beat you up once already.

—DONNIE, age 10

Kids on God and the Bible

Moses died before he ever reached Canada. Then Joshua led the Hebrews in the battle of Geritol.

The seventh commandment is thou shalt not admit adultery.

David was a Hebrew king skilled at playing the liar. He fought with the Finklesteins, a race of people who lived in Biblical times.

When Mary heard that she was the mother of Jesus, she sang the Magna Carta.

Jesus was born because Mary had an immaculate contraption.

The main difference between God and Jesus is that God has a white beard and Jesus has a brown one.

The people who followed the Lord were called the 12 decibels.

Jesus enunciated the Golden Rule, which says to do one to others before they do one to you. He also explained, "a man doth not live by sweat alone."

One of the oppossums was St. Matthew who was also a taximan.

An epistle is the wife of an apostle.

Three-year-old, Reese: "Our Father, Who does art in heaven, Harold is His name. Amen."

One particular four-year-old prayed, "And forgive us our trash baskets as we forgive those who put trash in our baskets."

A little boy was overheard praying: "Lord, if you can't make me a better boy, don't worry about it. I'm having a real good time like I am."

Facts According to Kids

Most of the houses in France are made of plaster of Paris.

An executive is the man who puts murderers to death.

A virgin forest is a forest where the hand of man has never set foot.

41

Johann Bach wrote a great many musical compositions and had a large number of children. In between he practiced on an old spinster which he kept in the attic.

The inhabitants of Moscow are called Mosquitoes.

A monsoon is a French gentleman.

The three elements of nature are sound, glitter, and glass.

Inflation is the material you put in your attic in the walls. It helps keep your house warm in winter.

Rainbows are to look at, not to really understand.

When you breathe, you inspire. When you do not breathe, you expire.

Floods in the Mississippi may be prevented by putting big dames in the river.

To most people solutions mean finding the answers. But to chemists solutions are things that are still all mixed up.

In the middle of the 18th century, all the morons moved to Utah.

Kids Embarrassing Parents

In a barber shop the other day a six-year-old came in alone, climbed up on a vacant barber chair and piped: "Give me a haircut like my Dad's—with a hole on top."

—ART LINKLETTER, entertainer and writer

At a restaurant one night, the waitress was sweet-talking my 5-year-old son, Josh. "Can I take you home with me?" she teased. Josh considered her proposal, then replied, "No, but you can take my dad. He snores, and he sleeps naked."

—Laura Christianson, quoted in *Parents* magazine

One recent morning, I overheard this poignant exchange between and father and his five-year-old son.

"I want my lunch," the boy proclaimed.

To which his father replied, "Well, how do you *ask* for it?"

"Like this: *I want my lunch.*"

—Bill Cosby, entertainer and writer

While at the doctor's office one day, my seven-year-old daughter said to the doctor, "Did you know that my mommy is older than my daddy?" To which I stammered a reply, "Oh, only by a few months."

—GWEN KELLY, mother of five

"What do you think your daddy does best?"
I asked one young man of five.
"Fall asleep in the chair," he replied.

—BILL COSBY, entertainer and writer

A small boy came home from his first day at Sunday school and began to empty his pockets of money—nickels, dimes, quarters—while his parents gasped in surprise. Finally his mother said, "Where did you get all that money?" "At Sunday school," replied the boy nonchalantly. "They have bowls of it."

—ART LINKLETTER, entertainer and writer

I was paying the admission fee for my five kids to enter an amusement park. The sign read, "Children 7 years and younger free." I told the ticket-taker that three of the kids would be free when one of my daughters piped up and said, "Daddy, I turned eight last month, don't you remember?"

—HOWARD KELLY, father of five

One day, my sister and her 5-year-old daughter, Hannah, saw a man with a tattoo that said "Mama." Hannah read it and said, "Mommy, he can't be a mama. He's a boy!"

—REBECKA LAMBERT, quoted in *Parents* magazine

People are quick to condemn you for the things you've done, but they'll never give you credit for all the times you resisted temptation.

—HEATHER, age 16

And what about the innocent who spouted: "My dad's a cop who arrests burglars, robbers and thieves." When I said, "Doesn't your mother worry about such a risky job?" he answered, "Naw, she thinks it's a great job. He brings home rings, and bracelets and jewelry almost every week."

—ART LINKLETTER, entertainer and writer

Kids' Wisdom

Love is the most important thing in the world, but baseball is pretty good too.

—GREG, age 8

Taking turns, that's just part of life.

—ANONYMOUS CHILD

The truth is the quickest and easiest way out of trouble.

—SARAH, age 12

It is OK to fail, but it is not OK to give up.

—KATE, age 8

What's something that grown-ups can learn from kids?

That we are different from them.

—CAROLINE, age 6

How to have fun and be wild!

—JUSTIN, age 4

Kids go to school so they can remind grown-ups about things they forgot.

—BAILEY, age 6

How to work the TV.

—EMILY, age 6

That a human has a head, thorax, and abdomen too.

—BROOKS, age 8

I think something grown-ups can learn from kids is don't be mean to other people.

—BEN, age 9

How to play dolls. How to pick out good clothes.

—LILY, age 9

The metric system.

—KAITLYN, age 10

Grown-ups can learn to loosen up once in a while or they'll never be happy.

—JESSICA, age 12

How to do a somersault. Or how to draw a picture.

—ANDREW, age 6

How to sing songs.

—BRENDAN, age 7

How to play like a kid.

—JIMMY, age 10

Patience.

—MICHAEL, age 15

Grown-ups should learn from kids that you only live one life. Live it to the fullest.

—CAMERON, age 15

Presidential facts.

—BENJAMIN, age 8

Chill out!

—KELSEY, age 8

Drawing with big crayons.

—GABRIEL, age 3

Stop and smell the roses every now and again.

—ALENA, age 8

Computer tricks.

—ARI, age 5

How to dance.

—ELIZABETH, age 12

How to have fun. When it's time to stop work and take a vacation.

—MICHAEL, age 8

What makes someone a good politician?

They take care of their country.

—KAITLYN, age 10

He tells everyone what to do.

—ANDREW, age 6

A good politician is someone who thinks they can be honest enough and stay honest enough to rule a nation.

—ALENA, age 8

Someone who is nice and easygoing.

—MADISON, age 9

A good politician is someone who understands what the people want and knows how to get it. They must have loyalty, determination, and be aggressive.

—CAMERON, age 15

They do a lot of speeches.

—CAROLINE, age 6

A good politician is involved with the community and is up-to-date with the issues.

—JESSICA, age 12

Getting up and clapping.

—SKYLER, age 3

A good politician is a person who lets the majority rule and lets the people help decide the laws.

—DILLON, age 10

Well, they represent everyone who they work for, and they do what they think is best for their town or country.

—JIMMY, age 10

A good politician is someone who is strong, won't go down without a fight. They like to argue. They are not afraid to look someone in the eye and tell the truth.

—MACKENZIE, age 10

Being smart and honest.

—PATRICK, age 11

When they were little they played games like apple bobbin. I bet they played that when they were little.

—KEVIN, age 5

Someone with strong beliefs who shows the people who they truly are and doesn't put on an act.

—MICHAEL, age 15

If they listen to all of the people and keep all of their promises.

—PETER, age 11

I think what makes a good politician is they respect the environment, they don't declare war on other countries just because of stupid reasons, and one who doesn't lie.

—BEN, age 9

Follow laws and make fair laws.

—KELSEY, age 8

If they grow whiskers.

—EMILY, age 6

They make the right choices.

—ALEXANDER, age 12

If they make good decisions and if they're nice to their country and if they keep their land healthy.

—LILY, age 9

How do you hope the world will change when you grow up?

Everyone will get to go to school. Every country will be a democracy.

—Jimmy, age 10

I hope there will be no terrorism.

—William, age 9

That everybody would have health and they won't be sick and they will never die.

—Rosie, age 6

All the kids will be bigger!

—Andrew, age 6

I hope the world will have lots of money, no more bullying, and that cars will have better gas mileage when I grow up.

—DILLON, age 10

Everyone is kind to each other and not have war.

—KAITLYN, age 10

I hope that we could destroy weapons of mass destruction without hurting people and that the prisons would not be so over crowded.

—ELIZABETH, age 12

I hope there will be more understanding and tolerance among cultures and people with different beliefs.

—MICHAEL, age 15

I want there to be a machine that I could use to pick if I have a boy or girl baby.

—EMILY, age 7

Pollution will decrease, no criminals, everyone is good.

—PATRICK, age 11

People will not be mad at each other. The world will be calm.

—JUSTIN, age 8

I hope there is a cure for cancer, no longer any racism, hate crimes, or terrorism.

—CAMERON, age 15

To have no bad guys or people stealing stuff or doing things the devil says.

—DANIELLE, age 5

No more littering and that they lower the fat in junk food.

—MADISON, age 9

When I am grown up I would like the world to be a nicer place, a place with less gigantic towering structures and more trees and grass and cars that run on solar energy and electricity and not nuclear reactors, and less people killing each other.

—BEN, age 9

That the world will be a safer place to live and have cool gadgets.

—KELSEY, age 8

I hope that God will answer all our prayers. I hope everyone has shelter, food, and a family to care for them. World peace.

—MACKENZIE, age 10

I hope there will be more cures for medicine and different ways to cure things than shots.

—MICHAEL, age 8

I hope the world will change with good daddies for me to marry.

—CAROLINE, age 6

I hope it will be peaceful.

—PETER, age 11

There will be a whole ozone again, and the Indians
will get their land back.

—BRENNA, age 11

That people wouldn't do bad stuff.

—BENJAMIN, age 7

If you had one wish, what would it be?

To have food and family and God looking over us.

—DANIELLE, age 5

Everything would cost one dollar.

—ARI, age 5

To have a million more wishes.

—WILLIAM, age 9

To draw a picture.

—JACK, age 4

To have everybody in my family right here.

—BAILEY, age 6

I would wish I were a dog, because then I would know all about dogs and humans.

—Avery, age 6

That my birthday would be every day.

—Emily, age 7

That people would live in a world without the kind of words we hear now.

—Elizabeth, age 12

To be the best that I can at whatever I do.

—Patrick, age 11

That I could eat ice cream every night.

—Caroline, age 6

To make the world a better place.

—KELSEY, age 8

That I could stay awake all night and never sleep.

—JUSTIN, age 4

Money.

—GABRIEL, age 3

That I didn't have to brush my teeth.

—BENJAMIN, age 7

That I could ride a shark.

—JUSTIN, age 4

I would wish for a giant roller coaster so I could ride it all day.

—CRISTIAN, age 6

I wish that I could fly like a bird.

—KEVIN, age 5

For everyone to be happy.

—MICHAEL, age 8

I hope that everyone is nicer to each other than they are now, especially kids. Being mean doesn't get you anywhere in life.

—JESSICA, age 12

The Wonder of Kids

As often as I have witnessed the miracle, held the perfect creature with its tiny hands and feet, each time I have felt as though I were entering a cathedral with prayer in my heart.

—MARGARET SANGER, nurse and writer

There is nothing more thrilling in the world, I think, than having a child that is yours, and yet is mysteriously a stranger.

—AGATHA CHRISTIE, novelist

You don't want to leave home in the morning and you can't wait to get home at night. She's a year and a half and she's changing all the time.

—JOHN GOODMAN, actor

Any adult who spends even fifteen minutes with a child outdoors finds himself drawn back to his own childhood, like Alice falling down the rabbit hole.

—SHARON MACLATCHIE, writer

A child is a being who gets almost as much fun out of a five-hundred-dollar set of swings as it does out of playing in a cardboard box or finding an earthworm.

—ANONYMOUS

When a child plays, he is the manipulator; he makes do with whatever is at hand. His imagination transforms the commonplace into the priceless. A wooden clothespin, rescued from under the kitchen table and wrapped in a dishcloth, becomes a baby; a penny thrust under a cushion becomes a buried treasure.

—EDA LESHAN, writer and educator

Play is often talked about as if it were a relief from serious learning. But for children play is serious learning. Play is really the work of childhood.

—FRED ROGERS, TV personality and educator

The illusions of childhood are necessary experiences: a child should not be denied a balloon because an adult knows that sooner or later it will burst.

—MARCELENE COX, writer

Kids are your standing excuse to indulge in all kinds of decidedly unadult behavior, like flopping down to make snow angels when the spirit moves you or speaking in a Donald Duck voice.

—PEG ROSEN, writer

Just the other morning I caught myself looking at my children for the pure pleasure of it.

—PHYLLIS THEROUX, columnist

One of the most delightful things about having children is experiencing the miracle of their development, watching the delight, innocence, and expression as they capture the newness in each experience, and sharing in the laughter of their play.

—ANNE K. BLOCKER, dietitian and writer

On viewing the Pacific Ocean for the first time, a four-year-old Kansas native exclaimed: "Look, Daddy—it just keeps flushing and flushing!"

—<small>ANONYMOUS</small>

You don't really understand human nature unless you know why a child on a merry-go-round will wave at his parents every time around—and why his parents will always wave back.

—<small>WILLIAM D. TAMMEUS</small>, columnist and writer

If a child is to keep alive his inborn sense of wonder, he needs the companionship of at least one adult who can share it, rediscovering with him the joy, excitement and mystery of the world we live in.

—<small>RACHEL CARSON</small>, biologist and writer

What silent wonder is waked in the boy by blowing bubbles from soap and water with a pipe.

    —RALPH WALDO EMERSON, writer and philosopher

The most sensitive, most delicate of instruments is the mind of a little child!

    —HENRY HANDEL RICHARDSON, writer

Every day you wake up to discover a slightly different person sleeping in that cradle, that crib, that bottom bunk, that dinosaur sleeping bag.

    —JOYCE MAYNARD, writer and journalist

Children are young, but they're not naïve. And they're honest. They're not going to keep awake if the story is boring. When they get excited you can see it in their eyes.

    —CHINUA ACHEBE, novelist

Having a young child explain something exciting he has seen is the finest example of communication you will ever hear or see.

—BOB TALBERT, WRITER

There are no seven wonders of the world in the eyes of a child. There are seven million.

—WALT STREIGHTIFF, writer

The monster under the bed finally arrived at our house the other night. I've been waiting for him to show up for four years.

—ANNA QUINDLEN, writer

There is a garden in every childhood, an enchanted place where colors are brighter, the air softer, and the morning more fragrant than ever again.

—ELIZABETH LAWRENCE, writer and columnist

Children display tremendous vitality and rush at every day with open arms.

—DR. DEEPAK CHOPRA, physician and writer

We find a delight in the beauty and happiness of children that makes the heart too big for the body.

—RALPH WALDO EMERSON, writer and philosopher

What Kids Teach Us

Anything which parents have not learned from experience they can now learn from their children.

—ANONYMOUS

If there were no other reasons (though we know there are as many as stars), this alone would be the value of children: the way they remind you of the comfort of simplicity. Their compelling common sense. Their accessibility and their honesty. Their lack of pretense.

—ELIZABETH BERG, writer

Level with your child by being honest. Nobody spots a phony quicker than a child.

—MARY MACCRACKEN, writer

It seems to me that since I've had children, I've grown richer and deeper. They may have slowed down my writing for a while, but when I did write, I had more of a self to speak from.

—ANNE TYLER, novelist

The more you listen to your child's ideas and values—even those with which you don't agree— the more likely it is that your child will listen respectfully to the ideas and values of others, including your own.

—LEE SALK, physician

I've learned that you should always take time to answer little children when they ask "why?"

—ANONYMOUS

In the effort to give good and comforting answer to the questioners whom we love, we very often arrive at good and comforting answers for ourselves.

—RUTH GOODE, writer

When we become parents, just being involved in our children's struggles evokes another reworking in us. *As parents, we have another chance to grow.* And if we can bring our children understanding, comfort, and hopefulness when they need this kind of support, then they are more likely to grow into adults who can find these resources within themselves later on.

—FRED ROGERS, TV personality and educator

We are given children to test us and make us more spiritual.

—GEORGE F. WILL, writer

You can learn many things from children. How much patience you have, for instance.

—FRANKLIN P. JONES, humorist

The thing you learn about children is that you can't change them.

—MICK JAGGER, rock star

If there is anything that we wish to change in the child, we should first examine it and see whether it is not something that could better be changed in ourselves.

—CARL JUNG, psychiatrist

Have a heart that never hardens, and a temper that never fires, and a touch that never hurts.

—CHARLES DICKENS, novelist

Our children teach us much more than we realize. Being a mother taught me patience, perseverance, self-discipline, and hard work. After coping for twenty-four hours a day with children, no task seemed too hard.

—MARY ANN KERWIN, writer and lawyer

Relish the time that you have with your child. Don't waste precious time feeling bad for moments you missed. Make the most of the here and now.

—ANNE K. BLOCKER, dietitian and writer

Don't get so involved in the duties of your life and your children that you forget the pleasure. Remember why you had children.

—LOIS WYSE, writer

As we get older it seems we lose faith in our ability to express ourselves as purely. Little children have a way of reminding us of our original purpose: joy.

—MARIE OSMOND, entertainer